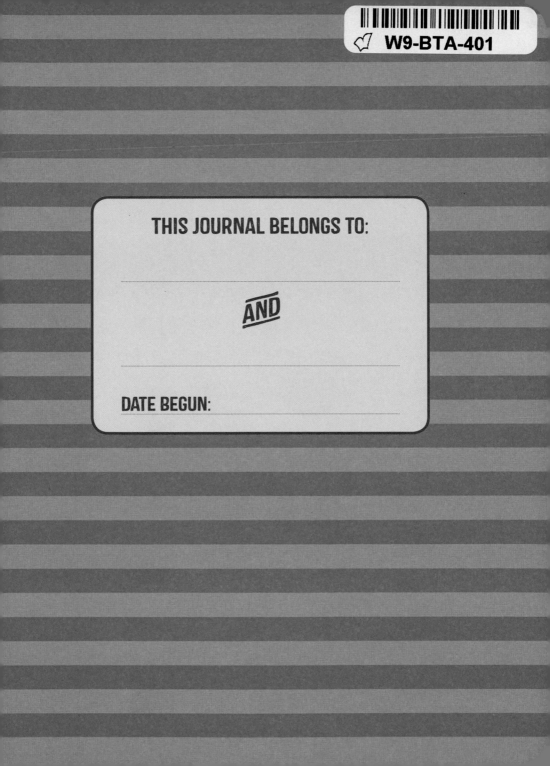

THIS JOURNAL BELONGS TO:

_____

AND

_____

DATE BEGUN: _____

MOTHER AND SON
OUR BACK AND FORTH JOURNAL

By Paula Spencer Scott

 PETER PAUPER PRESS, INC.
WHITE PLAINS, NEW YORK

FOR HENRY, NUMBER-ONE SON

PETER PAUPER PRESS
Fine Books and Gifts Since 1928

OUR COMPANY

In 1928, at the age of twenty-two, Peter Beilenson began printing books on a small press in the basement of his parents' home in Larchmont, New York. Peter—and later, his wife, Edna—sought to create fine books that sold at "prices even a pauper could afford."

Today, still family owned and operated, Peter Pauper Press continues to honor our founders' legacy of quality, value, and fun for big kids and small kids alike.

Designed by Heather Zschock
Map used under license from Shutterstock.com

Visit us at www.peterpauper.com

WHAT'S INSIDE

FOR MOTHERS:
Why a Mother-Son Journal?

Truth be told, my son didn't like to write. Not book reports, not made-up stories, not birthday or Mother's Day cards. Definitely not in a journal. Many kids don't.

Which is exactly why a journal like this one is great to have around.

All kids are different. Whether your son is a scribbler or more of a talker, or neither, or both, this journal is designed to turn small bits of writing time (and drawing time!) into fun for the two of you.

At its core, it's a connector. You, him, paper, time. Simple.

It's an easy way to get in some reading and writing. Kids need time to work on communication outside of school, and in a way that doesn't feel like homework. In this journal, the questions and prompts are written especially for boys. So he gets lots of chances to set words down on paper.

Because it's an interactive journal, it's also a fun way to find out about each other. Remember when he first learned how to talk? The youngest talkers tend to say whatever's on their minds at the moment, narrating the day as they go along. For me, that phase always felt like having x-ray vision into my kids' minds. But the older a boy grows, the harder it can be to get a handle on his opinions, ideas, likes and dislikes, and what makes him tick. Although this book purposely isn't a life-story journal (that might feel too much like homework), it is a snapshot of life right now. Through its range of activities and prompts, you'll learn a lot about one another's views, preferences, interests, and more. You can be sure that on some level he's curious about you, too. How are you alike? How are you different? So we built in plenty of opportunities for comparing responses.

It's a creative way to spend screen-free downtime together. And who's not looking for that?

It can also be a tool for expressing stuff that can be hard to talk about—from questions to complaints to mysteries of the boy universe, like: *What is so mesmerizing about that video game???* (And mysteries of the mom universe, too: *What do moms spend so much time talking to each other about?*) The prompts in this book aren't meant to put anyone on the spot. They're light and fun. But there are lots of jumping-off places for further conversation on all kinds of topics, as well as space for open-ended comments and more.

This journal can also become a fun keepsake of this moment in time.

What's on your minds right now won't be the same next year, or in five or 10 years. Interactive journals have a great double life: fun now, and fun to look back on later.

It might even turn into a starter kit for a lifelong habit of writing. I've kept a journal since I was nine years old. All it took was somebody handing me a blank book at that age, with a suggestion to get started.

Enjoy!

—*Paula Spencer Scott*

WAYS TO USE THIS BOOK
The only rule is . . . there are no rules!

SOME SUGGESTIONS:

Start at the beginning . . . or skip around.

You don't have to follow any particular order. Flip through some pages and start wherever piques your interest.

Go short . . . or go long.

Sometimes a three-word answer says it all. Other prompts invite a little more thought or imagination. It's all good. (And there's a whole section where all you have to do is make check marks!)

Do it together . . . or one at a time.

Some parts, like "Freaky Tales" and "Speed Ratings," make for fun side-by-side collaborations. Or you can take turns: First one of you fills in your part, marks the page, and then passes it to the other for his or her turn. Keep it for a few minutes or hours, or however you decide to do it. This journal is built for passing back and forth between you.

Take it on a trip.

Like a deck of cards or a trivia game, this interactive journal can pass the time when you're on a plane or in a car and want to give screens a rest.

Use it for school.

Sometimes teachers ask kids to keep a journal or do other daily writing exercises. When the assignment is open-ended, this kind of book can jump-start his thinking more easily than staring at page after blank page in a conventional journal.

Make it part of your bedtime routine.

One idea: Son picks an activity or prompt to do before he turns in, and marks the page. Then after he's asleep, Mom reads it and takes her turn so that he can look in the morning or the next evening. Back and forth. You get the drift.

Just be sure to do it in "green light" mode.

Did you know we all have an imaginary traffic light on our foreheads? When the light is red, we're just not receptive to other people. Maybe hunger or sleepiness is in the way. Maybe we're half-focused on something else. Maybe we're feeling overwhelmed by stuff going on. How can you tell when someone is in red-light mode? Once you get in the habit of looking, it's pretty easy! They're just not responding. (Mom, have you ever started peppering your son with questions the minute he arrived home . . . and gotten crickets back? Son, have you ever tried asking for something when Mom is sending an email?) But when that imaginary light is green—we're fed, rested, relaxed, devices off, in a good mood—it's way easier to talk, listen, and enjoy each other's company.

Above all . . . it's meant to be fun.

So feel free to cross out mistakes. Write big or write teeny-tiny. Try out some cursive or stick to good old printing. Use pencil or pen, in green or purple or red if you're so inclined. Nobody cares if the ink smears or the eraser leaves blotches, or a word gets misspelled along the way. (Got that, Mom?) It's your book.

Leave parts blank. Leave whole pages blank. Staple in extra pages. When you're all done, mark the date and save the whole thing for posterity.

Ready, set, go!

There's nothing like holding a fresh new journal in your hands and wondering what will wind up in there. Nothing, that is, except getting started!

LIKES

NAME AND COMPARE
YOUR FAVORITES, BESTS—

SOME STUFF YOU HATE.

★★★

LIKES

How are you two the same? How are you different?
Fill this out and compare!

	Mother	Son
BASIC FAVORITES		
Color		
Number		
Day of the week		
Time of day		
Month of the year		
Season		
Kind of weather		
Holiday		
Kind of pet		
Dog breed		
Dinosaur		
Wild animal		
Bug		
School subject		
Sport to play		
Sport to watch		

	Mother	Son
Sports team		
Song		
Mode of transportation		
T-shirt		
Item of clothing		
Musical instrument		
Store		
Restaurant		
Saying or slogan		

Mom's favorite hobbies:

Son's favorite hobbies:

	Mother	Son
FAVORITE FOODS		
Breakfast		
Cereal		
Lunch		
Dinner		
Dessert		
Snack		
Fruit		
Berry		
Veggie		
Nut		
Soup		
Cheese		
Movie-watching munch		
Pizza topping(s)		
Burger topping(s)		
Birthday cake		
Pie		
Cookie		
Candy		
Chips		

	Mother	Son
Crackers		
Pastry/donut		
Ice cream flavor		
Ice cream topping		
Drink on a hot day		
Drink on a cold day		
Spice		
Comfort food		
Ethnic food		
Celebratory meal		
Thing to cook		
Take-out order		
New food		
Smoothie		

FAVORITE PEOPLE & ANIMALS

	Mother	Son
Names for a pet		
Names for a person		

	Mother	Son
Relative		
Pro athlete		
Teacher		
Actor		
Actress		
Comedian		
Singer		
Band		
Other musician		
Author		
Cartoonist/illustrator		
President		
Historical figure		
Superhero		
Personal hero		
Comic book character		
Boy character in a book		
Boy character in a movie		
Mom character in a book		
Mom character in a movie		
Animal in a book		
Animal in a movie		

	Mother	Son
FAVORITE ENTERTAINMENT & FUN		
Kind of music		
Radio station		
Movie		
Comedy movie		
Scary movie		
Action movie		
Sci-fi/fantasy movie		
Animated movie		
TV show		
Game show		
Website		
Podcast		
App		
Video game		
Card game		
Board game		
Childhood book		
Recent book		
Book series		
YouTube video		

	Mother	Son
FAVORITE PLACES		
Town		
City		
State		
Country		
Vacation spot		
National park		
Other park		
Amusement/theme park		
Amusement park ride		
Museum		
Beach		
Pool		
Lake		
Place to run around		
Place to relax		
Hotel		
Room in our house		
Stadium		
Library		
Farm		

	Mother	Son
Farthest I've ever run		
Most sit-ups I can do		
Most push-ups		
Most pull-ups		
Highest thing I can reach		
Farthest I've traveled		
Number of states I've been in		
Longest I can hold my breath		
Coolest trick I can do		
Dream job		
Coolest car I've seen		
Childhood toy I won't toss		
Mom's weirdest dream		
Son's weirdest dream		

	Mother	Son
A FEW OTHER THINGS	**Make your own favorites to compare!**	

FOR SON:

Best way to spend $1

Best way to spend $10

Best way to spend $100

Best ways to spend $1 million

Best present I ever got

Best present I ever gave

Best way to cheer me up

FOR MOTHER:

Best way to spend $1

Best way to spend $10

Best way to spend $100

Best ways to spend $1 million

Best present I ever got

Best present I ever gave

Best way to cheer me up

MOM'S *favorite way to spend a summer afternoon*

SON'S *favorite way to spend a summer afternoon*

MOM'S *favorite way to spend a Saturday morning*

SON'S *favorite way to spend a Saturday morning*

MOM'S *favorite way to hang out with the family*

SON'S *favorite way to hang out with the family*

★ ★ ★

AND SOME DISLIKES...

	Mother	Son
Household chore I hate		
Trend I hate		
Least favorite time of day		
Least favorite food(s)		
Least favorite holiday		
Worst movie I ever saw		
Worst book I ever read		
Habit I wish I could break		
Habit I wish you could break		
Hardest thing about current school grade		
Least favorite school subject		
Hobby I'll never try		
What I hate most about winter		
What I hate most about summer		

MOM'S *instant mood destroyer*

SON'S *instant mood destroyer*

MOM: *Most annoying thing my son says or does*

SON: *Most annoying thing my mom says or does*

Thing ***MOM*** *hates for people to say*

Thing ***SON*** *hates for people to say*

MOM'S *pet peeve about where we live*

SON'S *pet peeve about where we live*

MY FIRSTS

	Mother	Son
Pet		
Trip away from home		
Team sport played		
Uniform number		
Riding a bicycle		
Movie I saw in a movie theater		
Video game I played		
Book I read by myself		
Day of school		
Teacher		
Friend I remember		
Plane ride or road trip (where to?)		
Thing I bought with my own money		
Job (or big responsibility)		

YOUR TURN, MY TURN

ANSWER THESE
BURNING QUESTIONS.

There's space to come up with
some of your own, too.

10 THINGS
SONS WANT TO KNOW
(Mom, have at it!)

1. Why do you have so many rules?

2. What do you remember most about being my age?

3. What is your life like when I'm in school?

4. What do moms talk about when they get together?

5. What did you think the first time you saw me?

6. What did you like about being a kid?

7. If you were a kid today, do you think you'd like it?

8. Is being a mom hard?

9. Can you read my mind or do you just fake it?

10. If you could do anything for a day, what would it be?

10 THINGS
MOTHERS WANT TO KNOW
(Son, have at it!)

1. Explain what's so great about your favorite game.

2. What's the most annoying rule you have to live by—and why is it annoying?

3. What do I do that embarrasses you?

4. What's your idea of the perfect birthday?

5. What is sooooo funny about gross sounds? Explain!

6. Do you wish you had more siblings or fewer siblings?

7. What rule would you make for me, if you could?

8. If you could rewind a day you'd like to do over, how would it be different?

9. Which grade of school has been the best so far, and why?

10. Which of your stuff do you want me to save forever?

Here are some you both get to answer. How do you compare?

FOR SON...

You're stranded on an island with three other people. Who would you choose?

1.

2.

3.

Describe yourself in three words:

1.

2.

3.

Okay, now describe ME in three words:

1.

2.

3.

Who should play you in a movie about your life, and what would the movie be called?

Who should play ME in a movie about my life, and what would the movie be called?

What kind of animal would you be, if you could pick? Why?

If a genie gave you one wish, what would you wish for?

What kind of aliens do you think are out there?

If you could live at any time in history, when would it be and why?

What's the best knock-knock joke you've heard?

What makes you nervous?

What would be different if you were a billionaire?

What do you like best about our house?

FOR MOTHER...

You're stranded on an island with three other people. Who would you choose?

1.

2.

3.

Describe yourself in three words:

1.

2.

3.

Okay, now describe ME in three words:

1.

2.

3.

Who should play you in a movie about your life, and what would the movie be called?

Who should play ME in a movie about my life, and what would the movie be called?

What kind of animal would you be, if you could pick?

If a genie gave you one wish, what would you wish for?

What kind of aliens do you think are out there?

If you could live at any time in history, when would it be and why?

What's the best knock-knock joke you've heard?

What makes you nervous?

What would be different if you were a billionaire?

What do you like best about our house?

MAKE UP YOUR OWN

Come up with your own questions,
and answer them!

QUESTION:

Mom's answer:

Son's answer:

QUESTION:

Mom's answer:

Son's answer:

QUESTION:

Mom's answer:

Son's answer:

TRY THIS!

WHO SAID JOURNALS HAVE TO BE FULL OF SENTENCES?

This section mixes it up with
a bunch of different ways to
express yourselves.

A COMIC ABOUT
THE WORLD'S FREAKIEST ROBOT

A COMIC ABOUT
THE WORST DAY EVER

A COMIC CALLED

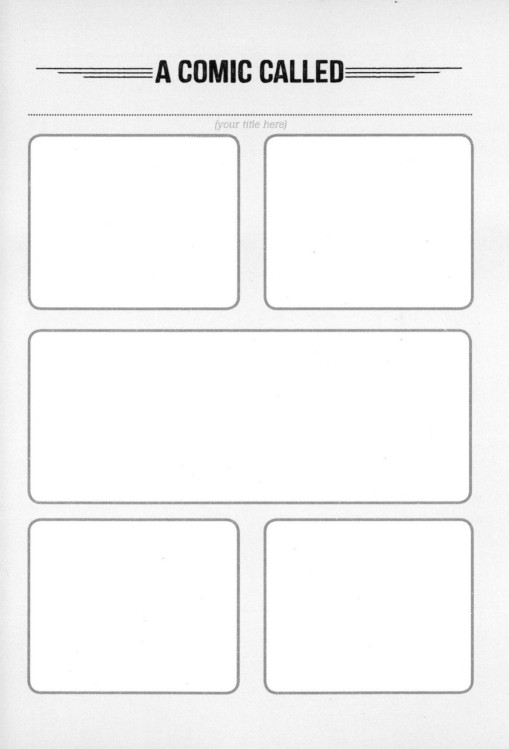

MY SIX-WORD LIFE STORY

MOM: ....

....

ILLUSTRATE IT

SON: ....

....

ILLUSTRATE IT

CREATE YOUR OWN ICE CREAM FLAVOR

(One catch: It can't really exist yet!)

MOM'S

What's it called?

What's in it?

What color is it?

How do you make it?

Any special toppings?

SON'S

What's it called?

What's in it?

What color is it?

How do you make it?

Any special toppings?

BUILD THE PERFECT FORT/GETAWAY

MOTHER'S

What's it made out of?

Where is it?

Give it a name:

What's inside it?

What happens there?

USE THIS SPACE TO DRAW IT

SON'S

What's it made out of?

Where is it?

Give it a name:

What's inside it?

What happens there?

USE THIS SPACE TO DRAW IT

INVENT THE NEXT BIG THING

MOTHER'S

What's your invention called?

What does it do?

How does it work?

Who uses it?

USE THIS SPACE TO DRAW IT

SON'S

What's your invention called?

What does it do?

How does it work?

Who uses it?

USE THIS SPACE TO DRAW IT

PUT ON A DISGUISE

MOTHER'S

What's the overall look?

Is there a hat or head-covering?

Is there anything different about your face?

Do you have a secret name?

Do you have a special accent?

Where do you wear this disguise?

USE THIS SPACE TO DRAW IT

SON'S

What's the overall look?

Is there a hat or head-covering?

Is there anything different about your face?

Do you have a secret name?

Do you have a special accent?

Where do you wear this disguise?

USE THIS SPACE TO DRAW IT

DISCOVER A NEW LIFE FORM

MOTHER'S

What's it called?

Where did you find it?

What does it look like?

What can it do?

Does it speak or make sounds?

What will happen to it?

SON'S

What's it called?

Where did you find it?

What does it look like?

What can it do?

Does it speak or make sounds?

What will happen to it?

USE THIS SPACE TO DRAW IT

LET'S PLAY
LITERAL DIRECTIONS

Here's how it works: One of you writes down instructions for how to do something—step by step. Then the good part: You read it out loud while the other person follows the instructions exactly.

(Warning: It's trickier than it sounds!)

FIRST MOTHER: *Tell how to put on a sweater, step by step.*

NOW SON: Tell how to make your favorite sandwich, step by step.

DESCRIBE OR DRAW THE CAR OF YOUR DREAMS HERE.

MOM'S DREAM RIDE

SON'S DREAM RIDE

PROCLAIM A NEW HOLIDAY!

MOTHER'S

What's it called?

When is it?

What's being celebrated?

What happens on that day?

Is any special food involved?

Are there any special decorations or clothes?

SON'S

What's it called?

When is it?

What's being celebrated?

What happens on that day?

Is any special food involved?

Are there any special decorations or clothes?

WHERE WE'VE BEEN

List all the places you've traveled to and what
you liked (or didn't) about each place.

MOTHER

Destination	Liked / Didn't like

SON

Destination	Liked / Didn't like

DREAM DESTINATIONS

List all the places you'd like to travel to.
Put a star next to the places you'd like to travel to together.

Mother	Son

WHAT WE LIKE TO DO ON VACATION

Check all that apply!

	Mother	Son
Swim in the ocean		
Swim in a pool		
Lounge on the beach		
Read a book		
Take a scenic hike		
Ski or snowboard		
Visit a museum		
Go on amusement rides		
Have a spa day		
Camp		
Shop for souvenirs		
Try new food		
See a show		
Visit a landmark		
Go on a boat ride		
Take a tour		
Make a sand castle		
Go fishing		

WE CAN BE HEROES

MOTHER'S SUPERHERO IDENTITY

Your superhero name:

Your special power:

Name of the movie about you:

Other superheroes you'd like on your team:

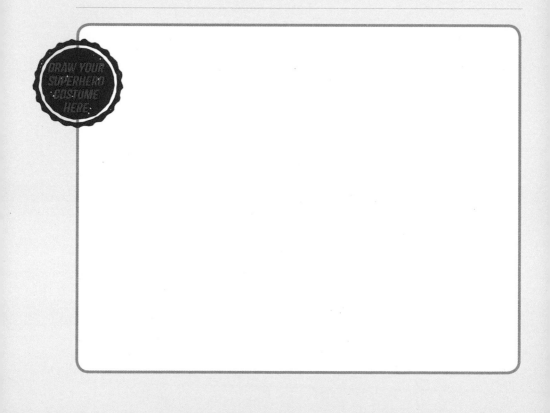

DRAW YOUR
SUPERHERO
COSTUME
HERE.

SON'S SUPERHERO IDENTITY

Your superhero name:

Your special power:

Name of the movie about you:

Other superheroes you'd like on your team:

DRAW YOUR SUPERHERO COSTUME HERE

A TIMELINE OF OUR GREATEST HITS

Mark some of the best and biggest days you remember.

MOTHER'S TIMELINE

The day I
was born
_____

SON'S TIMELINE

The day I
was born
_____

Today

Today

SECRET MESSAGES
Write a message in secret code.

MOTHER TO SON:

SON TO MOTHER:

THE SECRET CODE:

A=N B=O C=P D=Q E=R F=S G=T H=U I=V J=W K=X L=Y M=Z

N=A O=B P=C Q=D R=E S=F T=G U=H V=I W=J X=K Y=L Z=M

Write a message using your favorite emojis.

MOTHER TO SON:

SON TO MOTHER:

FREAKY TALES

YOU WRITE A SENTENCE; I WRITE A SENTENCE.

WHERE THE STORY ENDS UP IS ANYBODY'S GUESS!

Mother writes on the orange lines;
Son continues the story on the blue lines; then
keep taking turns to see where your tale goes.

IF DOGS HAD CELLPHONES

THE DAY MOM QUIT

THE ZOMBIE NEXT DOOR

DIARY OF A PIRATE'S REALLY BAD DAY

I WAS TRAPPED IN A VIDEO GAME

And Now, Two True Stories!
MY LIFE SO FAR: MOTHER'S STORY

"I was born in _____. I've heard that I

looked like _____. Supposedly I got my

name because _____. My earliest memory is the

time _____. The song I remember

best from when I was young is _____.

My first favorite toy was _____.

As a little kid, I liked to _____.

I will always remember my mom telling me, '_____

_____.'

My favorite thing to do as a little kid was _____.

I dreamed of being a _____ when I grew up.

I feel _____ about how

things are turning out so far. What I really like to do best with my time is

_____. If I could pick one

thing to make my life better it would be _____.

Next year, I wish I could _____.

All in all, I'm a _____ person."

SON'S STORY

"I was born in _____. I've heard that I

looked like _____. Supposedly I got my

name because _____. My earliest memory is the

time _____. The song I remember

best from when I was younger is _____.

My first favorite toy was _____ .

As a little kid, I liked to _____.

I will always remember my mom telling me, '_____

_____,'

My favorite thing to do as a little kid was _____ .

I dreamed of being a _____ when I grew up.

I feel _____ about how

things are turning out so far. What I really like to do best with my time is

_____. If I could pick one

thing to make my life better it would be _____.

Next year, I wish I could _____.

All in all, I'm a _____ person."

SPEED RATINGS

QUICK!
GIVE YOUR
GUT REACTIONS.

You can do these pages together or answer
separately and then compare. Count up how
many things you have in common—or not!

THIS OR THAT?

Check the box next to the thing you think is better!

Mother	Son
☐ Chocolate milk or regular milk ☐	☐ Chocolate milk or regular milk ☐
☐ Slimeball or paintball ☐	☐ Slimeball or paintball ☐
☐ Dogs or cats ☐	☐ Dogs or cats ☐
☐ Comedy or horror ☐	☐ Comedy or horror ☐
☐ Light sabers or saber tooth tigers ☐	☐ Light sabers or saber tooth tigers ☐
☐ Math or English ☐	☐ Math or English ☐
☐ Minecraft or Legos® ☐	☐ Minecraft or Legos® ☐
☐ Godzilla or Tyrannosaurus rex ☐	☐ Godzilla or Tyrannosaurus rex ☐
☐ Roller coaster or race car ☐	☐ Roller coaster or race car ☐
☐ Phone or computer ☐	☐ Phone or computer ☐
☐ Acoustic guitar or electric guitar ☐	☐ Acoustic guitar or electric guitar ☐
☐ Space travel or time travel ☐	☐ Space travel or time travel ☐
☐ Camping or hotel ☐	☐ Camping or hotel ☐
☐ Silly string or silly putty ☐	☐ Silly string or silly putty ☐
☐ Aquarium or terrarium ☐	☐ Aquarium or terrarium ☐
☐ Bath or shower ☐	☐ Bath or shower ☐
☐ Thunder or lightning ☐	☐ Thunder or lightning ☐
☐ Vanilla or chocolate ☐	☐ Vanilla or chocolate ☐

Mother	Son
Convertible or SUV	Convertible or SUV
Xbox® or PlayStation®	Xbox® or PlayStation®
Checkers or chess	Checkers or chess
Shorts or jeans	Shorts or jeans
Knights or pirates	Knights or pirates
Graphic novels or comic books	Graphic novels or comic books
Pancakes or waffles	Pancakes or waffles
Sunrise or sunset	Sunrise or sunset
Rock skipping or rock throwing	Rock skipping or rock throwing
Pretzels or potato chips	Pretzels or potato chips
Microscope or telescope	Microscope or telescope
Skateboards or bikes	Skateboards or bikes
Jellyfish or jelly roll	Jellyfish or jelly roll
Climbing trees or climbing walls	Climbing trees or climbing walls
Broccoli or Brussels sprouts	Broccoli or Brussels sprouts
Painting or spray painting	Painting or spray painting
Star Wars or Star Trek	Star Wars or Star Trek
Cake or cookies	Cake or cookies
Checkers or chess	Checkers or chess
Monday or Friday	Monday or Friday

HOW MANY STARS?

Son first: Circle or color in the number of stars (from 1 to 5, with 5 being the highest) that you think your mom would give the following . . . then let Mom fill in her side or tell her answers out loud, and see what she really thinks.

	Son's Guess for Mom	Mom's Real Answer
Bungee jumping	★ ★ ★ ★ ★	★ ★ ★ ★ ★
Zip-lining	★ ★ ★ ★ ★	★ ★ ★ ★ ★
Self-driving cars	★ ★ ★ ★ ★	★ ★ ★ ★ ★
Coffee	★ ★ ★ ★ ★	★ ★ ★ ★ ★
Slime	★ ★ ★ ★ ★	★ ★ ★ ★ ★
Running a marathon	★ ★ ★ ★ ★	★ ★ ★ ★ ★
Bubble baths	★ ★ ★ ★ ★	★ ★ ★ ★ ★
Selfies	★ ★ ★ ★ ★	★ ★ ★ ★ ★
Mud	★ ★ ★ ★ ★	★ ★ ★ ★ ★
Vacuuming	★ ★ ★ ★ ★	★ ★ ★ ★ ★
A woman president	★ ★ ★ ★ ★	★ ★ ★ ★ ★
Texting	★ ★ ★ ★ ★	★ ★ ★ ★ ★
Rock music	★ ★ ★ ★ ★	★ ★ ★ ★ ★
Country music	★ ★ ★ ★ ★	★ ★ ★ ★ ★
Rap music	★ ★ ★ ★ ★	★ ★ ★ ★ ★
Classical music	★ ★ ★ ★ ★	★ ★ ★ ★ ★

	Son's Guess for Mom	Mom's Real Answer
Hip-hop	☆ ☆ ☆ ☆ ☆	☆ ☆ ☆ ☆ ☆
Jazz	☆ ☆ ☆ ☆ ☆	☆ ☆ ☆ ☆ ☆
My singing	☆ ☆ ☆ ☆ ☆	☆ ☆ ☆ ☆ ☆
Staying up late	☆ ☆ ☆ ☆ ☆	☆ ☆ ☆ ☆ ☆
Sleeping in	☆ ☆ ☆ ☆ ☆	☆ ☆ ☆ ☆ ☆
Scuba diving	☆ ☆ ☆ ☆ ☆	☆ ☆ ☆ ☆ ☆
Tattoos (in general)	☆ ☆ ☆ ☆ ☆	☆ ☆ ☆ ☆ ☆
Tattoos (on you)	☆ ☆ ☆ ☆ ☆	☆ ☆ ☆ ☆ ☆
Watching the World Cup	☆ ☆ ☆ ☆ ☆	☆ ☆ ☆ ☆ ☆
Watching the Olympics	☆ ☆ ☆ ☆ ☆	☆ ☆ ☆ ☆ ☆
Watching cartoons	☆ ☆ ☆ ☆ ☆	☆ ☆ ☆ ☆ ☆
Watching reality shows	☆ ☆ ☆ ☆ ☆	☆ ☆ ☆ ☆ ☆
Going to Mars	☆ ☆ ☆ ☆ ☆	☆ ☆ ☆ ☆ ☆
Lizards as pets	☆ ☆ ☆ ☆ ☆	☆ ☆ ☆ ☆ ☆
Cockroaches	☆ ☆ ☆ ☆ ☆	☆ ☆ ☆ ☆ ☆
Clowns	☆ ☆ ☆ ☆ ☆	☆ ☆ ☆ ☆ ☆
Riding a camel	☆ ☆ ☆ ☆ ☆	☆ ☆ ☆ ☆ ☆
Camping	☆ ☆ ☆ ☆ ☆	☆ ☆ ☆ ☆ ☆
Clothes shopping	☆ ☆ ☆ ☆ ☆	☆ ☆ ☆ ☆ ☆
Grocery shopping	☆ ☆ ☆ ☆ ☆	☆ ☆ ☆ ☆ ☆

Now Mom's turn: Circle or color in the number of stars (from 1 to 5, with 5 being the highest) that you predict your son will answer . . . then ask him for his answers and see what he really thinks.

	Mom's Guess for Son	Son's Real Answer
Bungee jumping	☆ ☆ ☆ ☆ ☆	☆ ☆ ☆ ☆ ☆
Zip-lining	☆ ☆ ☆ ☆ ☆	☆ ☆ ☆ ☆ ☆
Self-driving cars	☆ ☆ ☆ ☆ ☆	☆ ☆ ☆ ☆ ☆
Coffee	☆ ☆ ☆ ☆ ☆	☆ ☆ ☆ ☆ ☆
Slime	☆ ☆ ☆ ☆ ☆	☆ ☆ ☆ ☆ ☆
Running a marathon	☆ ☆ ☆ ☆ ☆	☆ ☆ ☆ ☆ ☆
Bubble baths	☆ ☆ ☆ ☆ ☆	☆ ☆ ☆ ☆ ☆
Selfies	☆ ☆ ☆ ☆ ☆	☆ ☆ ☆ ☆ ☆
Mud	☆ ☆ ☆ ☆ ☆	☆ ☆ ☆ ☆ ☆
Vacuuming	☆ ☆ ☆ ☆ ☆	☆ ☆ ☆ ☆ ☆
A woman president	☆ ☆ ☆ ☆ ☆	☆ ☆ ☆ ☆ ☆
Texting	☆ ☆ ☆ ☆ ☆	☆ ☆ ☆ ☆ ☆
Rock music	☆ ☆ ☆ ☆ ☆	☆ ☆ ☆ ☆ ☆
Country music	☆ ☆ ☆ ☆ ☆	☆ ☆ ☆ ☆ ☆
Rap music	☆ ☆ ☆ ☆ ☆	☆ ☆ ☆ ☆ ☆
Classical music	☆ ☆ ☆ ☆ ☆	☆ ☆ ☆ ☆ ☆
Hip-hop	☆ ☆ ☆ ☆ ☆	☆ ☆ ☆ ☆ ☆
Jazz	☆ ☆ ☆ ☆ ☆	☆ ☆ ☆ ☆ ☆

	Mom's Guess for Son	Son's Real Answer
My singing	★★★★★	★★★★★
Staying up late	★★★★★	★★★★★
Sleeping in	★★★★★	★★★★★
Scuba diving	★★★★★	★★★★★
Tattoos (in general)	★★★★★	★★★★★
Tattoos (on you)	★★★★★	★★★★★
Watching the World Cup	★★★★★	★★★★★
Watching the Olympics	★★★★★	★★★★★
Watching cartoons	★★★★★	★★★★★
Watching reality shows	★★★★★	★★★★★
Going to Mars	★★★★★	★★★★★
Lizards as pets	★★★★★	★★★★★
Cockroaches	★★★★★	★★★★★
Clowns	★★★★★	★★★★★
Riding a camel	★★★★★	★★★★★
Camping	★★★★★	★★★★★
Clothes shopping	★★★★★	★★★★★
Grocery shopping	★★★★★	★★★★★

★★★

TRUE OR FALSE?

	Mother		Son	
There's no such thing as too many video games.	T	F	T	F
I wish I could speak three more languages.	T	F	T	F
Gotta catch 'em all.	T	F	T	F
Walt Disney was a genius.	T	F	T	F
Shakespeare was a genius.	T	F	T	F
I have faked a stomach ache.	T	F	T	F
I am a spy. (Don't tell anyone.)	T	F	T	F
I care if my socks match.	T	F	T	F
Actions speak louder than words.	T	F	T	F
I wish I could pitch a no-hitter.	T	F	T	F
I wish I could run a triathlon.	T	F	T	F
Elephants never forget.	T	F	T	F
Kids used to have more fun than they do now.	T	F	T	F
You should kiss grandmas hello.	T	F	T	F
I would like to be five again.	T	F	T	F
Humans will get to Mars in my lifetime.	T	F	T	F
I like to read.	T	F	T	F
I like to sleep.	T	F	T	F
Spiders have six legs.	T	F	T	F

SPEED ANSWERS

Take turns: One asks the questions aloud and writes down the other's answers.

MOTHER ASKS:

Quick! How many planets can you name?

How many oceans can you name?

If you could make me read one book, what would it be?

What's the last nice thing you did for someone?

Can you name five words that start with the letter Q?

What did you dream about last night?

What were you thinking just this second?

SON ASKS:

Quick! How many mountains can you name?

How many rivers can you name?

If you could make me read one book, what would it be?

What's the nicest thing I ever said to you?

Can you name five words that start with the letter Z?

What did you dream about last night?

What were you thinking just this second?

BIG PLANS

THINGS TO DO,
PLACES TO GO,

and a spot to keep track of them all.

A PACT

Let's make time to do something fun together
every month—just the two of us.

30 STARTER IDEAS
Borrow away!

- Before-school diner breakfast
- A matinee movie—or a really late show
- Sample a different ice cream parlor every month
- Go apple-picking (or pick another in-season crop)
- Take turns choosing a TV series to binge-watch
- Teach ourselves a new card game
- Papier-mâché something
- Volunteer at a soup kitchen
- Enter a run/walk race
- Tie-dye T-shirts
- Study optical illusions
- Surprise a neighbor by doing something nice
- Go horseback riding
- Watch the entire "Star Wars" or "Harry Potter" series
- Go fishing

- Plant a tree or a garden
- Learn Morse code
- Help on a campaign
- Have a museum day
- Rent a tandem bike
- See a pro sporting event we've never been to
- Attend a concert or theater show
- Get binoculars and go bird watching
- Learn how to tie three different knots
- Dare to take up whittling
- Tour local government offices
- Build a tree house, snow fort, or similar structure
- Learn CPR
- Visit a planetarium or go star-gazing
- Start a canned food drive, coat drive, or similar effort

COLLABORATE:

Brainstorm ideas together!

Some things we could cook together:

Causes we could champion:

Ways we could raise money for charity:

Good deeds we could do for neighbors:

Some things we could learn how to do:

Great places for a day trip:

Movies we should watch together:

Books we should read together:

Any rules we should have for "our time"?

Examples: We take turns picking the event. We make it the same day every month or the same day of the week. Nobody else is allowed. Ice cream is always on the agenda. (Or whatever works for you two!)

WHAT WE DID

(a monthly fill-in record)

JANUARY

FEBRUARY

MARCH

APRIL

MAY

JUNE

JULY

AUGUST

SEPTEMBER

OCTOBER

NOVEMBER

DECEMBER

SOME PLANS FOR NEXT YEAR!

TRAVEL BRAINSTORMS: Mom's Ideas

Places I'd love to fly to

Places I'd love to drive to

A perfect family vacation

Ideas for a great stay-cation

TRAVEL BRAINSTORMS: Son's Ideas

Places I'd love to fly to

Places I'd love to drive to

A perfect family vacation

Ideas for a great stay-cation

LET'S PLAN A DREAM ADVENTURE

Where we should go:

When we should go:

Who we should invite:

How we should get there:

What we should do there:

Audiobooks we should listen to:

Snacks for the road:

Stuff we can't travel without:

Souvenirs to hunt for:

Pictures to take:

Map, GPS, or no plan at all?

What would be great about traveling with you:

What might not be so great about traveling with you (sorry!):

OUR BUCKET LIST

18 things we should do together before the big 18th birthday

	Mother	Son
1		
2		
3		
4		
5		
6		
7		
8		
9		
10		
11		
12		
13		
14		
15		
16		
17		
18		

MOTHER'S thoughts on how we should celebrate high school graduation:

SON'S thoughts on how we should celebrate high school graduation:

A CLOSING NOTE

You made it! To wrap up this journal,
write each other a closing note.

MOTHER'S NOTE:

SON'S NOTE:

PAULA SPENCER SCOTT is the author of the guided journals *An Oral History: Preserve Your Family's Story* and *Like Mother, Like Daughter: A Discovery Journal for the Two of Us* (with her daughter, Page Spencer). Her other books include *Surviving Alzheimer's: Practical Tips and Soul-Saving Wisdom for Caregivers*. She has one son, two stepsons, and three daughters. She writes often about family and health, and has kept a daily journal since age nine.

★ ★ ★